This field guide & journal is the property of

_____

Kirnell Publishing

2023

ISBN: 979-8-9890645-0-2

A Well-Seasoned Woman's

Field Guide & Journal

Prompts & Inspiration for Your
Personal Discovery & Self-Care

by

Kathleen Davis

dedication

For all of the perfectly imperfect
women who make up my community,
past. present, and future...

Because of you, I have been changed for good.

how to use this field guide & journal

I designed this field guide & journal to be used in a way that feels good to you. Period. That's it.

So...

Maybe you'll develop a system for working your way through the field guide & journal, or maybe you'll make it up as you go.

Maybe you'll designate a specific time of day as "journal time," or maybe you toss the field guide & journal in your bag and pull it out whenever and however the opportunity for journaling presents itself throughout the day.

Maybe you'll break out colored pens, magazine pictures, & a glue stick to embellish your responses, or maybe you'll scrounge for some kind of writing utensil in the console of your mini-van, counting yourself lucky to find a half-chewed pencil.

Guess what? This field guide & journal was meant for all of the above and more. It's meant to be a sacred, safe space that can be accessed right where you are, right in the midst of the beautiful,messy,awkwardness of your real life.

My only hope? That this resource gets at least a little bent & stained, with your handwriting going both inside & outside the margins--chock full of what you're capturing about yourself and about Life itself as you delve into what's waiting for you inside. xo

See page 146 for more on journaling as a mental health support.

Allowing each season of life
to flow easily into the next
on purpose
is the work of a

Well-Seasoned Woman

"To everything, there is a season, and a time to every purpose under heaven."

King Solomon & the Byrds

Maiden Seasoning

"I now affirm the blossoming of my unique creative potentials."

Sometimes, we simply need to toot our own horn a bit.

What are 4 things you *positively love* about yourself?

Some songs are just made for dancing.

What songs are part of your personal DANCING QUEEN playlist?

Circle all the things you wanna do more often.

buy flowers

wear lipstick

get crafty

eat dessert

Try a new hairstyle

travel internationally

lose yourself in a book or film

flirt

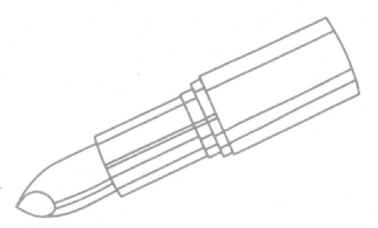

take a different
route home

lie in the grass

strike up a
conversation with
someone new

try a new
cuisine

dance

get lost on purpose

say yes

take a class in
something totally
unexpected

We all have something that makes us afraid. For some it might be driving someplace new while others might fear the thought of speaking in public.

What is something you feared but did anyway? How did you feel afterwards?

"*Feel* the fear, and do it anyway."

Eleanor Roosevelt

Losing ourselves in what *fascinates* us is one of Life's

most *delicious* invitations.

The "just one more page" of a new book that turns into an all-night read-a-thon. The planned quick stop by the new artsy boutique that turns into an hours-long linger.

What are some of the things that still cause you to *lose yourself* in time & space?

Experimenting
with our dreams
&
taking risks
always costs
us something.

But we've gotta keep
reminding ourselves--
we're
worth
every penny
of the investment.

"Paris is always a good idea,"
shared the fictional
character Sabrina, in the
film named for her. It
seems some things are
always a good idea.

What is always a good idea for you?

"Take chances, make mistakes. That's how you grow.

Pain nourishes your courage.

You have to fail in order to practice being brave."

--Mary Tyler Moore

Applying a new kind of makeup for the first time, cooking an untried recipe without a picture of what the finished dish should look like, impulsively volunteering for the new project--we often learn more from simply jumping in than we do from following a familiar, more ordered way of doing things.

WHAT IS SOMETHING YOU'VE LEARNED THE MOST ABOUT FROM JUST *jumping in* **AND DOING IT?**

Capture your thoughts, doodles, sketches, clippings, &/or favorite quotes/poems here.

I welcome
the new with

open arms

&

enjoy
expanding

my
comfort zone.

There are many versions of what **BRAUE** looks like. *Sometimes, it's a physical action; sometimes it's an emotional risk; sometimes it's a mental shift.*

Describe a time recently when you were brave.

What did you discover about *yourself?*

Each of us has some quirky skills that are noteworthy among our family & friends.

Perhaps we're the one others call when a jar needs opening, a movie title needs remembering, or a demonstration of how to pick up a paper clip with our toes needs displaying.

What are some of your uniquely quirky skills?

Learning new things keeps us flowing in life.

What topics are you interested in learning more about?

" Go to some place where you can see the sky, and walk up and down a little."

Teresa of Avila

Going on a road trip can be a ton of fun, allowing us to discover new places and have unexpected encounters with people and/or nature.

CREATE A TOP TWENTY LIST OF THE SONGS, SNACKS, &/OR PERSONAL ITEMS THAT WOULD HAVE TO BE AVAILABLE IN THE CAR IN PLANNING FOR YOUR ULTIMATE ROAD TRIP.

35

always playing
it safe

perfectionism

constant
assumption-making

body shame

the same old
same old, all the time

leading with
no

rigidity

holding shame
over honest errors

Cross out what you're ready to release.

holding back

constant apologizing

refusing to consider new options

declining offers to play

never ending rule-following

non-stop comparing

the need to always be certain

mean people

While watching new movies is an adventure, it's the films we return to *again & again* that frequently hold the most meaning for us.

Create your personal "Best Movie Marathon"
list, including 5-15 of your all-time
favorite titles.

Mother Seasoning

"My work is my gift to the world and I delight in the fruits of my labor."

What's something you're working on now that you're taking great *delight* in?

Circle the messages you'd most like to hear from a person you love/respect.

I love you
exactly as you are.

You deserve
joy.

I see you.

To me, you are
perfectly imperfect.

I believe
in you..

I love your mind.

No matter what,
I'm on your team.

I trust you.

Your body
is gorgeous.

I totally approve
of who you are.

Now, consider speaking at least
one of the messages you chose
every morning, noon, and night to
the woman in the mirror.

Select a fictional mother
from your favorite book, or movie, or
TV series to have dinner with.

Whom do you choose and why?

"O most honored Greening Force,

You who roots in the Sun;
You who lights up, in shining
serenity, within a wheel
That earthly excellence fails
to comprehend.

*You are enfolded
in the weaving of divine mysteries.*

You redden like the dawn
And you burn: flame of the
Sun.

Hildegard von Bingen

What is your formula for the perfect summer day?

Consider including "ingredients" that
can be seen, tasted, touched/felt, heard,
& sniffed appreciatively.

We all have things
we take pride in.
For some, it's a
physical skill,
while others savor
their mental prowess
or their emotional
connections.

What are some of the things you take pride in?

"Everything on Earth began with her, grew out of her, and will return to her.

This is *Mother Earth* as a womb and tomb, personified as the Great Mother of ancient and indigenous peoples:

Our *Mother*, who art the *Earth*."

--Jean Shinoda Bolen

Capture your thoughts, doodles, sketches, clippings &/or favorite quotes/poems here.

Maybe it's that text exchange you have with a longtime friend. Perhaps it's that phone call from a family member. Or, it could be that unplanned chat you had with the friendly grocery clerk or your next door neighbor. Whatever and whenever they happen, small connections with other people and pets are full of benefits.

1

2

3

4

5

6

7

8

9

10

11

12

13

14

15

16

For the next 31 days, list small, positive connections you experience with another person, group, or animal-- either planned or spontaneous.

17	18	19	20
21	22	23	24
25	26	27	28
29	30	31	

There are many versions of what PERSEVERING looks like.

Sometimes, it's a physical action. Sometimes, it's a prolonged, emotional hoping. Sometimes, it's a mental hanging on.

Describe a time recently when you chose to **persevere**. What did you discover about *yourself?*

Summer is the time and season of growth, abundance,& fruition-- both for Mama Nature & wherever in our own seasonal cycling the *fruits of our labor* appear.

Circle all that speaks to you of Life's ripening yumminess &/or the taste of sweet success.

sweet corn

wild blueberries

truly meaningful work

fresh

green beans

just-baked peach pie

contributing to the greater good

recognition of my efforts

vine-ripened tomatoes

juicy
watermelon

crispy,
fried
okra

holding the
diploma

nailing the
interview

tender
cantaloupe

homemade
ice cream

meeting the
goal

cucumber
water

strawberry
shortcake

freshly
picked
lavender

Design your
dream work space using
whatever works--*words,
sketches, &/or glued-in
magazine photos.*

Some of our most *satisfying* relationships are not with other humans, but with the animals, pets, and plant life.

Write about a "nonhuman" relationship you have now or have had in the past.
How is your life *richer*

because of this relationship?

It's often the small, ordinary gestures that make us feel the most connected to & loved by others.

An emptied dishwasher, an "I love you" scribbled on a napkin, a piece of your favorite chocolate left on your pillow, a lavish compliment paid in front of friends, or a small gift "just because"--

What are some of the small, ordinary things that make you feel the most loved & valued?

I savor the beautiful, messy, & awkward imperfection of reality, relationships, & me.

Think about a project/challenge you took on and saw it through to the end.

What contributed to your ability to stick with it? How did it feel once it was complete?

Cross out what you're ready to release.

Always sacrificing my preferences & needs

Waiting for someone else to meet my needs

Hiding my light under a bushel

Fearing that my effforts are meaningless

Saying no to all social invitations

A scarcity mindset

Belief that everything should come easily

Trying to be it all, all at once

Holding back

Giving up on myself

Saying No to Joy

Being scared to speak up on behalf of others

Allium

While I did not fix
the thing I most
wish to fix, and I
did not do
the most important
thing on my list,
and I did not save
anyone, and I did
not solve the world's
problems, I did
plant the onion sets
in the garden,
pressed my fingers
into the dry earth,
knew myself as
a thin dry start.
Oh patience, good
self. This slow
and quiet growing,
this, too, is
what you are
here to do.

Rosemerry Wahtola Trommer

Write about a person or group you love now that you could never have imagined loving in the past.

What about you or them changed enough to allow for love to ripen?

Matriarch-Queen
Seasoning

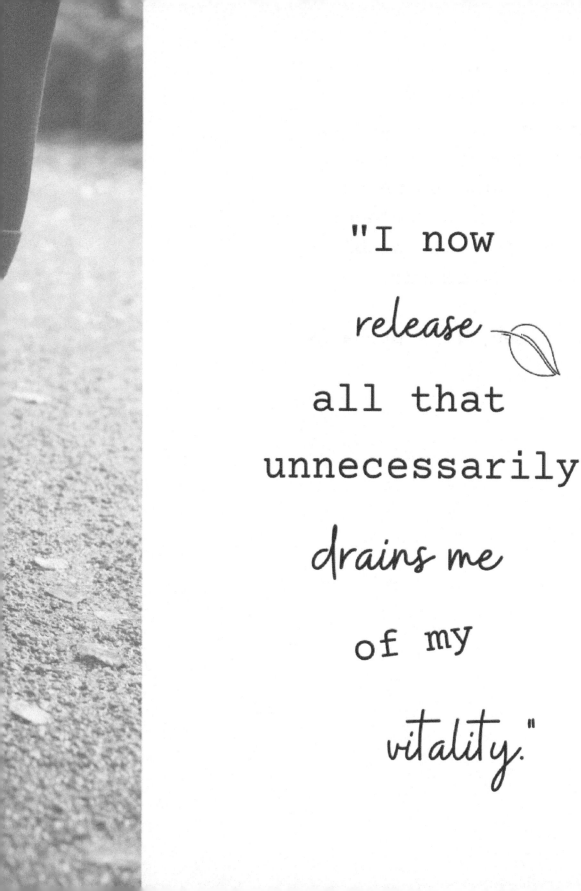

"I now *release* all that unnecessarily *drains me* of my *vitality.*"

Letting go of a responsibility, a relationship, or a role can be really hard; but other times, we are so *ready* for the release that we feel measurably lighter afterwards.

Most times, it's probably a *bit of both*.

Write about a time when *stepping back* was both a little hard but also at least a little bit of a relief.

Which of these absolutely needs to be tattooed, either permanently or temporarily, onto your body right now? Why?

I am enough

beauty matters

Don't look back; you're not going that way.

love never fails

just breathe

fear not

let go

I am not responsible for your opinion of me

Use pp.82-83 if more room is needed to
record your thoughts.

good things
take time

do all with love

When a feather
appears, loved
ones are near.

just keep
swimming

Dream. Plan. Do. Rest.

as the sun,
we will rise again

resist much;
obey little

only kindness
matters

let it be

She thought
she could,
so she did

Success isn't about getting more things done; it's about investing your *time & energy & strength* in what is worthwhile.

As of right now, what are some of the things that *matter most to you?*

It's probably pretty easy to think about the things that are going wrong, but what are some of the things that right now feel abundant and full of goodness?

Capture your thoughts, doodles, sketches, clippings, &/or favorite quotes/poems here.

An electrical current
knows nothing of the path
it will take. It follows all paths,
but flows best toward
where it flows best.
It sounds so simple,
and yet the electrons of this body,
charged with my beliefs,
defy nature and rush toward resistance.
How often I try to fight myself.
How often I battle my own current,
the current of the world—
it's like wading through honey instead of water,
this thinking I know best.
Sometimes, I see how my own resistance
is nothing but a part of the path.
In that moment, I flow toward where I flow best.
In that moment I am copper, ductile, tough,
In that moment, I am so alive with it, the buzz.

Turning to Physics

Rosemerry Wahtola Trommer

This or That: Circle One

PUMPKIN LATTE OR PUMPKIN CARVING

LEAF PILE JUMPING OR FALL ROAD TRIP

SCARECROW OR TIN MAN

TOMATO PIE OR SQUASH CASSEROLE

COSTUME PARTY OR TRICK 'R TREATING

APPLE CIDER OR APPLE CIDER DONUTS

CORDUROY JACKET OR CROCHETED BLANKET

CANDY CORN OR CORN MAZE

WITCHY FORTUNE TELLING OR BARN DANCING

COZY MYSTERY OR TERRIFYING TALE

BONFIRE OR CANDLELIGHT

"I'm so glad to live in a world where There are Octobers."

Anne Shirley, as written by
L.M. Montgomery

As time moves forward, we discover that we are constantly being invited to shift with it. New technology, new neighbors, updated work expectations, family fluctuations — all evolve with time.

What is a change you might
have resisted at first but are
now making in order to keep up
with Life's ongoing buzz?

Woman with Flower

I wouldn't coax the plant if I were you.

Such watchful nurturing may do it harm.

Let the soil rest from so much digging

And wait until it's dry before you water it.

The leaf's inclined to find its own direction;

Give it a chance to seek the sunlight for itself.

Much growth is stunted by too careful prodding,

Too eager tenderness.

The things we love we have to learn to leave alone.

Naomi Long Madgett

There are many versions of what Letting Go looks like. Sometimes, it's a **physical** action; sometimes it's an *emotional* detachment; sometimes it's a **mental** dismissal.

Describe a time recently when you chose to *Let Go*. What did you discover about yourself?

Maybe it was that time you let your 9-year old niece take credit for cooking the holiday stuffing that you mostly created. Maybe it was the time you filled out the *Employee of the Month* nomination for a co-worker.

Write about a time when you let someone else **shine.**

Just for fun, let's imagine a genie in a bottle is offering you 24-hours worth of unlimited use of his magic carpet.

Where will you go? What will you do?

"Each season of life flows into the next as easily as I allow it to happen."

Cross out what you're ready to release.

putting myself last

resisting my quiet inner knowing

ignoring my body's wisdom

fearing that nothing ever changes

fearing that everything is changing

repressing & suppressing

staying busy so I don't have to think

feeling like I'm living someone else's life

hating my today body

staying small to appease that scolding inner critic

being anti-aging instead of pro-aging

resisting compliments

The Latin phrase,
dulcius ex asperis,
translates into
"sweeter after
difficulty."

Write about an experience you've had that you found sweeter after navigating the difficulty associated with it.

Circle what you'd like to experience more of right now...and really, every single day.

being authentic

music

Tea

genuine laughter

sunsets

day dreaming

making generous assumptions

yumminess

acting on my
longings

long walks

sidewalk
cafes

signing my own
permission slip

saying what
I truly feel

books

full moons

giving & receiving
compliments

kindness

WHAT 3 TO 5 PIECES OF ADVICE ABOUT LIFE OR YOUR JOB OR A ROLE YOU HOLD WOULD YOU MOST LIKE TO PASS ON TO "UP-AND-COMERS"--THOSE WHO ARE YOUNGER AND/OR WITH LESS EXPERIENCE?

When good things happen, instead of chalking it up to "random luck," we need to recognize that our thoughts and actions played a part in leading us to our reward.

What good thing have you received recently that you can recognize you attracted by your intentional choices?

Sometimes, we receive feedback that something we've said made a *real difference* for someone else.

What is one thing you've done or said that someone told you made a difference *for the good* in their lives?

"To be a presence of perpetual **thanksgiving** may be the ultimate goal of life.

The **thankful person** is the one for whom life is simply one long exercise in the *sacred*."

Sister Joan Chittister, OSB

Taking stock of our resources from time to time can be an invaluable exercise.
List where/ to whom you turn when you need...

Comfort

Unconditional support

Excitement

Laughter

Honest feedback

Playtime

Inspiration

Courage

Which resources do you have in abundance?
Which resources could use some enhancing?

Crone Seasoning

"I intuitively

&

intentionally

surrender

to

winter's ❄

(re)newing

power."

What ingredients simply must be included in concocting your perfect Winter Day?

When we are overextended, depleted, and/or overstimulated, taking the time to notice and draw upon the foundational elements that comprise our most basic of needs can provide real comfort & renewal.

1	2	3	4
5	6	7	8
9	10	11	12
13	14	15	16

For the next 31 days, take note of a person, place, thing, activity, or ritual that you discover supports your wellness, your home's coziness, your financial security, and/or your sense of loving comfort.

17	18	19	20
21	22	23	24
25	26	27	28
29	30	31	

When his mother died in 2005, Charlie McBride decided that etching his mother's favorite peach cobbler recipe on her gravestone was a uniquely personal tribute, honoring her gifts.

What recipe or "How To" instructions would you consider worthy of being etched into your gravestone one day? Why did you choose what you did?

~~Cross out~~ all the things you're
especially ready to say good-bye to:

~~Bitterness~~

Resisting change

Body blaming & shaming

Toxic positivity

Rigidity

Overspending

Raging at aging

Resentment

Burnout

Chronic busyness

Ignoring my body's distress signals

Discounting my dreams

Fear related to slowing down

Most of us enter adulthood with inherited beliefs about money-- many of them negative.

What is one belief about money that you've chosen to adopt that is different from & more positive than those you inherited?

How is your life better because of this choice?

(Circle) all the things that you need to bring more cozy, reset time into your life.

spend time in nature

have unproductive fun

savor stillness

pillow fight

give myself permission to not be helpful

record more dreams

light more candles

go unplugged

dance
under the
stars

make a
snow angel

sleep

embrace silence

be a little wild

gather around
the fire

snuggle
under a blanket

look at life
with the eyes
of a child

Much of our practical wisdom in life is hard-won; we know what we know because we had to learn it by first experiencing it as difficult, messy, & awkward.

Write about a piece of
hard-won *wisdom*
you now possess because
you learned it the
hard way.

☐ ☐ ☐ ☐

Throw a penny in the
wishing well.

*What are you wishing
for right now?*

Life isn't about me; I am about **Life.**

As a child, many of us were convinced that without the nightlight, the monster under the bed or in the closet might get us.

What about now? What is your relationship with the dark? Is it still scary, or has it evolved into something different?

Mycelial

Now I understand how grief
is like a mushroom—
how it thrives in dark conditions.
How it springs directly
from what is dead.
Such a curious blossoming thing,
how it rises and unfurls
in spontaneous bourgeoning,
a kingdom all its own.

Like a mushroom,
most of grief is never seen.
It grows and expands beneath everything.
Sometimes it stays dormant for years.

Grief, like a mushroom,
can be almost unbearably beautiful,
even exotic, delicate, veiled,
can arrive in any shape and hue.
It pulls me closer in.

Like a mushroom, grief
asks me to travel to regions
of shadow and dim.
I'm astonished by what I find—
mystery, abundance, insight.
Like a mushroom, grief
can be wildly generative.
Not all growth takes place
in the light.

Rosemerry Wahtola Trommer

Sometimes, we choose to forgive another person—not in order to move forward with the relationship, but--as a way of *moving forward* with our lives.

Write about a person or situation you have forgiven or are in the process of forgiving because you realize it's *simply time* to move on.

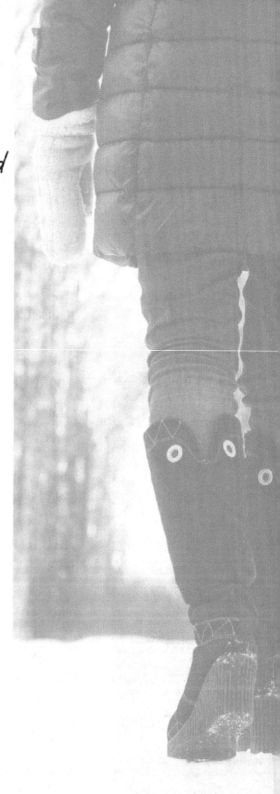

This or That: Circle One

HOT CHOCOLATE OR MULLED WINE

BRAND NEW BOOK OR OFT-READ NOVEL

HEIRLOOM QUILT OR WEIGHTED BLANKET

TOMATO SOUP OR CHICKEN NOODLE SOUP

SOCKS OR SLIPPERS

FULL MOON OR DARK MOON

SKIING OR SLEDDING

SNOWING OR SUNNY & COLD

CHOCOLATE OR PEPPERMINT

KNEE BOOTS OR ANKLE BOOTS

MITTENS OR GLOVES

CANDLES OR TWINKLE LIGHTS

Noticing how we begin our mornings can transform how we experience our entire day.

What personal morning practices have you discovered set you up for experiencing a terrific day?

While a funeral is frequently the most solemn of experiences, those that include smiling or even laugh-out-loud remembrances of the loved one often provide deep comfort in the midst of grief.

What are some joyful, quirky and/or zest-filled things about your life & your story that you suspect might be shared amongst your loved ones after you're gone?

"Our mother's zest and passion *for life,* her children, grandchildren and her many animals, not to mention her eternal joy in creating, were unparalleled and leave us inspired to live life to the fullest just as she did."

--statement released by Kirstie Alley's family shortly after her death in December 2022

Capture your thoughts, doodles, sketches, clippings, &/or favorite quotes/poems here.

Imagine that you're watching a really engaging film that stars a woman whose life & values are identical to yours.

What challenges must she overcome to achieve her dreams? How does she go about figuring out her next steps? What are your biggest inspirational take-aways about her?

Perhaps it was a grandmother or great-grandmother. Perhaps it was a woman at work or church or from the neighborhood.

Write about an older woman who greatly influemced you for good. What about her most inspired you?

Although we continue to grow and change, which of your personal, childlike qualities do you hope to always possess?

endnotes

Mother Seasoning

"Everything on earth began with her" is reproduced by permission from Jean Shinoda Bolen, Like a Tree: How Trees, Women, and Tree People Can Save the Planet (San Francisco, CA: Conari Press, 2021).

"Allium" is reproduced by permission from Rosemerry Wahtola Trommer. All the Honey (Samara Press, April 18, 2023).

Matriarch-Queen Seasoning

"Turning to Physics" is reproduced by permission from Rosemerry Wahtola Trommer, A Hundred Falling Veils (blog post). April 23, 2021. https://ahundredfallingveils.com/2021/04/23/turning-to-physics/

"Woman with Flower" by Naomi Long Madgett is reproduced by permission. The Garden Thrives: Twentieth –Century African-American Poetry, edited by Clarence Major. (New York: HarperCollins Publishers, 1996).

"To be a presence of perpetual thanksgiving" quote on p. 107 by Sister Joan Chittister, OSB, is reproduced by permission.

Crone Seasoning

"Mycelial," track 3 on Rosemerry Wahtola Trommer and Steve Law's Dark Praise electronic album, Sweet Tooth Sound, 2023 is shared with permission.

The Well-Seasoned Woman's Studio

The Well-Seasoned Woman's Studio is an online community that's all about empowering & supporting women through *The Well-Seasoned Woman's Newsletter*, blog posts, and (coming soon) online course modules, as we explore questions such as:

- *When will I stop over-functioning and under-living?*
- *How can I shift from being anti-aging to being pro-aging?*
- *What does it mean to honor and express my creative inklings?*
- *When will I truly recognize the woman staring back at me in the mirror?*
- *How can I make friends with ch-ch-ch-change?*
- *When will I know I am enough? Will I ever be enough?*

In the Well-Seasoned Woman's Studio, we practice working WITH the deep goodness of our primal rhythms and drives—something most of us were never taught; but as a woman learns to say YES to her natural, biological wiring, it's like she's adjusting her sails to work with the wind, and she can't help but notice how much more easily every part of her voyage flows.

You can learn more & sign up to receive *The Well-Seasoned Woman's Newsletter* at www.KathleenDavis.com

writing as a self-care, mental health practice

My cross-generational and racially diverse community is filled with women who are spunky and kind, thoughtful and industrious. These women move mountains for the people they love and the causes they support, but they often find themselves challenged--as so many of us do-- in focusing any of their loving super-powers on themselves.

As it turns out, a journal is a terrific place to begin practicing self-discovery and authentic self-care, especially when the journal is designed to also be a field guide, one meant to help each woman filter through the noise and unwelcome advice of others and (re)discover the goodness of her own voice, her own life, and her own natural rhythms.

I believe that any effort we make at slowing down long enough to get in touch with our preferences, our longings, & our inner knowing, and to experience our primal connectedness-- both to our bodies and to the natural world around us-- is a very good thing indeed, contributing to our wellness, and by extension, the wellness of those in our communities.

It feels like a small but very doable sort of practical magic-- one that research* continues to support. xo

*Read more about journaling research in my blog at www.KathleenDavis.com

about the author

Kathleen Davis is a content creator, certified holistic coach, workshop leader, and originator of the Well-Seasoned Woman's Studio.

She's also a wife, mom, gigi, friend, and long-time Southern Maryland resident who seeks to live into the truth that, "to everything, there is a season, and a time to every purpose under heaven," one messy, awkward, imperfect, and often humorous step at a time.

Connect with Kathleen directly via email:
Kathleen@KathleenDavis.com

Follow Kathleen on social media
- Face Book: The Well-Seasoned Woman's Page
  https://www.facebook.com/KathleenDavisWSW/
- Instagram @kathleengdavis

www.KathleenDavis.com

Because this is your time,
your life, your season.
Why not do it on purpose?

Made in the USA
Coppell, TX
23 October 2023

23249305R00083